Selected Poems by George Coombs

George Coombs

authorHOUSE

AuthorHouse™ UK Ltd.
500 Avebury Boulevard
Central Milton Keynes, MK9 2BE
www.authorhouse.co.uk
Phone: 08001974150

© 2009 George Coombs. All rights reserved.

No part of this book may be reproduced, stored in a retrieval system, or transmitted by any means without the written permission of the author.

First published by AuthorHouse 8/26/2009

ISBN: 978-1-4490-1036-2 (sc)

This book is printed on acid-free paper.

Introduction

THIS IS A SELECTION of my poetry from the past ten years. The poems come from experience, thought and feeling and will, I hope, give my readers food for their own thought and reflection. I have been writing poetry for many years and it has always been a natural form of expression and statement for me. I have written stories, articles and two novels and am an artist yet poetry is a first and lasting love.

The poems are grouped as 'Nature' 'Mum and Dad' and 'Conflict.' Each section is preceded by an example of my artwork and the cover design is mine

I have always loved nature and the idea of being one with all creation. Being close to the created order has often inspired expressions of peace and tranquility yet also concern regarding intrusion into that peace believing that man is merely a strand in the web of life and that as he harms to web he harms himself.

My parents, elder brother and indeed other members of my close and extended family have now passed into the next life. I remember them all. The poems in this group are mainly linked to my late mother as indeed, they would be yet Dad and Aunty Eve (Dad's sister) are also represented.

Mum was wheelchair disabled with arthritis and I was her carer and companion for many years. I have many memories of her courage, good humour and concern for others while coping with great pain and adversity. Mum's passing was initially devastating and only gradually have I been able to go on taking Mum and indeed many loved friends and family in the next life with me.

Then there is conflict. Not only the kinds of personal conflict that proliferate in human experience but conflict within the social order. I am presently writing a book, which tells the story of my activities trying to help people in prison or hurt by the system in any way. The book will be called 'Justice? – You Decide' So welcome to my book. There will also be examples of my art that, together with my poetry will, I hope cause readers to pause and think. This is my purpose of everything as a writer and artist.

George Coombs

Nature

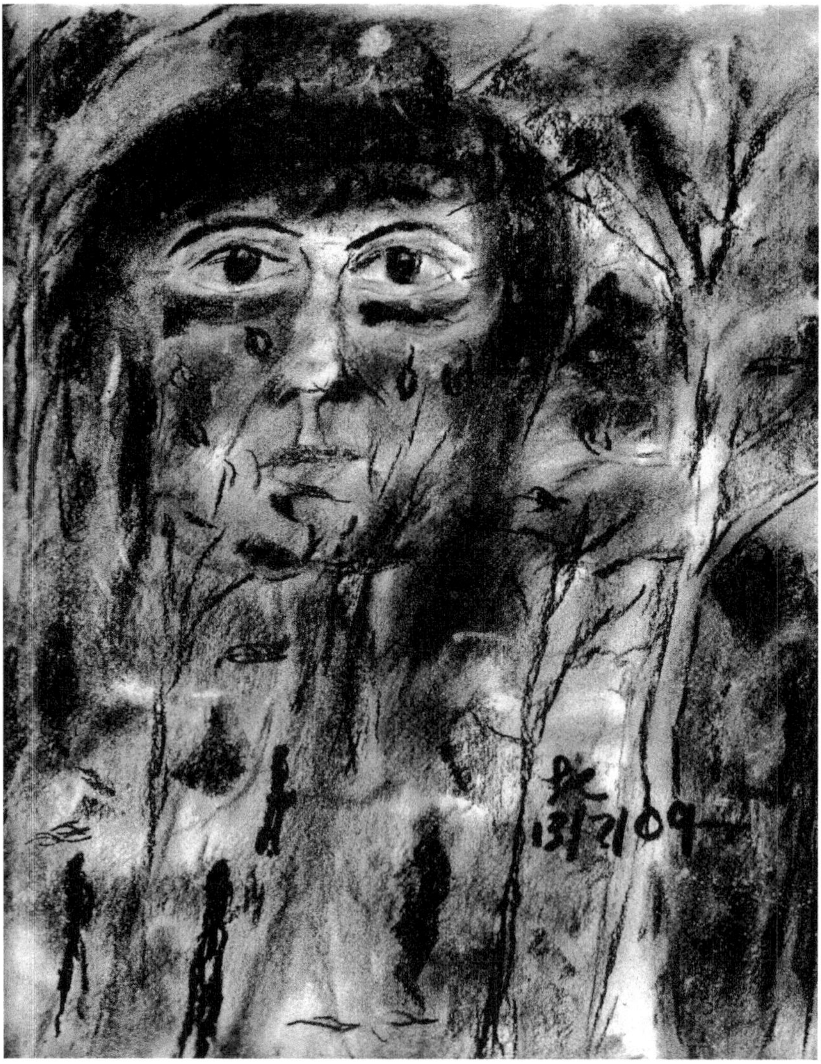

A New Creation

Gull cries
Pulsates in fading light
Good to hear
Heralding of created vastness,
Song of distant
Horizon where the searching
Question yearns
For refuge in everlasting truth.

A moment
Ageless and eternal
New creation
Where the mind could roam
In innocence
Aware of the one life where
Through all that gathers
Runs the shining cord of truth.

Autumn Afternoon

A time for looking
Trees yearn upward
Branches wave like
Beckoning hands
Fragile leaves scattered
Over the grass.
Mind can be still
Floating on rivers
Of autumn wind
To farthest horizons
Of untravelled existence.
Memories call down the years
Now I welcome them
I can listen here where
A gull calls across the sky
Heralding vastness, need for
Space to grow into the light.

Autumn Midnight

*Autumn night
Here, my walking
Footfalls are slow
Pulse in gathered darkness*

*Dim illumination
Haunts deserted streets –
Trees beckon
Gentle*

*In quiet wind
Church like hush
Noise only
Within the self*

*Life falls here
Among frail
Leaves, human
Vulnerability*

*Here where
Autumn softly
Touches
Gently cold*

*Midnight,
Walking in
Space between
Light and darkness*

*Between day
And night
Nobody here
It is all vast*

Like the mind
That holds
The way of
Searching

Here, in this
Long moment
Freedom
From terror

Of being touched
Here, truly alive
Walking slowly, great joy
In being alone

Children

New creation
Here, in the leaf carpeted
Park in autumn.
Trees rustle in rivers of wind
Squirrels, birds
Children running innocent
As light
Sprinkling the air
With joy and laughter
Running, playing, climbing
Bodies gilded in
Autumn brightness.
I watch now,
Distant from them
While furtive steps move
Along their life path.

Day in Autumn

Sitting
Looking
Again the scene
Park carpeted with
Fallen leaves frail
As humanity
Trees vein shadowed
Sky with agonized
Contorted architecture
Here
Now
Desolation leading to
Re-creation, a new birth
In the one-ness of all life
Starting again
Knowing here, this day
In autumn
There is a way to peace.

From Here

From here the window
Offers trees, fields still
Under the early morning sky.
The lake glass like
Reflects sunlight through clouds.

Gentle sense of vastness,
Oneness of all created life
Touches my eyes
Sense of beyond light
Waits a vast unending light.

Bird song sprinkles country air, all
Life listens aware, aware of
New creation vast and innocent
Here in calm and stillness gathering
The newly awakened longing mind.

Gathered Shade

No fear
Of being touched
Here
In a Church garden

Plants, flowers
Trees with reverently
Bowed branches
Tremulous

In gentle
Streams of wind
Coming
To my space

Like an
Anointing hand.
Part of oneness
Of all creation

Here in
The gathering shade
Part of oneness
Of all creation

Here in
The gathering shade
Safety,
Free at last in
The gathering shade.

GULL

Quietly gilded
In early evening light
The Gull
On my
Window ledge

I often
Hear their call
Heralding
Sky vast as
The mind

Cry to look
Up and beyond
Where questions
Float free as
Bubbles in the breeze

Sea is near,
Horizon, a better
Way awaits
The traveler robed
In wisdom

With ever outstretched hand
Now we share a
Quiet where we
Are together in
In the one life.

Holding Silence

I hold silence
Close in the heart
Needing refuge
From interior noise
I walk slowly
Feeling a gathering
Hush, sense of the unearthly
Here in the innocent
Bird anthemed morning.

Modest foliated trees
Are symbols of yearning
For truth and clear seeing.
Ripples roam the lake,
Tremulous strings offering
Music to my waking eyes,
Sense of oneness of all life,
Whispers of light unending

On My Sofa

On my sofa,
Early morning, I
Find quietness,
Stillness as in
An empty Church
Where one senses
Refuge, a place of peace.

Ticking of the clock
Like reverential footsteps
Slowly walking the path
Of the truth seeker.
Gulls hymn newly created
Day, light enters quietly,
Touch of cool air is

A wise hand inviting
Me into this present
Moment where all I
Can offer here, in this
Real divine abiding
Is myself quietly aware
In this moment where all is well.

Poem in Autumn

Skeletal trees
Vein the grey sky.
I walk in leaf carpeted
Quietness feeling safe
In each new moment.
Nature now fragile,
Vulnerable as personhood.

Pebble in limpid pool
Of quietness,
Vast rippling vibrations
This is one-ness of
All created life
Gathering here where
I can be still and know.

Resting

Sprinkled on quietness
Bird's song
Welcomes newly created
Light here this gentle morning.

Resting in the present moment.

Good to be one,
To be whole here
In safety
Where light quietly comes.

Resting in the present moment.

Thinking of those
Now entered the endless shining
Needing no concept
Of time in realms of true freedom

Resting in the present moment

Calmly wanting
Clear seeing ancient and ageless.
End of betrayal and fear
Beginning of gathering

Resting in the present moment.

Share the Morning

Eyes touched with morning
Gulls chant over this
Still river of quiet.
Sense of being free...
New created existence
No internal noise,
Violation of the person
Seeking to look
With clear eyes
Above forests of the
Unquiet self.
In stillness undisturbed
Sense of those
Frail minds vulnerable
Like fallen leaves
Scattered where
Morning vibrates with
Doors heavy like crushing ignorance.
One must be strong
Allowing call of Gulls to look up
Prison will never work –
Darkness proliferate
In collective consciousness
Shadow is between punishment
And not doing it again
We share the morning
With the question "Why?"

Snow

Slow, silent snow
Settled softly where
Winter trees veined a
Pigeon grey sky.
A quiet space
Where cold penetrated
Like a searching question.
Me, here as still
White wanderers drift
Slow and inevitable.
Now, as often, waiting
Aware of seasons turning,
For all things comes a time.

Spider

Slow, silent
Sinister stealth
Between leaves
Constructing
Survival dependent
Silvern architecture
Supported by
Space the web
Evolved
As I wandered
In the
Early morning.
Life needs
Space in which to
Live
Nothingness between
Pillars
Supports the
Tall building.
Here, reality
Of thought as
The web
Evolved slowly like
A worked
Out concept.
Here too
Spirit of inevitable
Predator waiting
For the fly vulnerable
As humanity.
Yet spider centered
In the web waiting,
Observing is
Harmless when
Allowed to be
Alive and still.

The Path

Walking quietly
Where the paths lay before
Me lined with emaciated
Winter trees
Aware of silence allowing
Thought to range free
As the Gull, cry filling
A vast overarching sky
Frail leaves litter waiting ground
Displaced, vulnerable as
Human life; bird's nature
Survive and change with time
Yet the path to walk is always there
Birds are nature's voice beckoning
To look even though a grey sky through
Skeletal branches obscure the sun

Time

*Branches
Tremulous in rivers
Of quiet wind.
Leaves litter soft
Ground here
Where I find*

*Time of quiet
Breathing new air.
For all that is
Created a time.
Life is here
Moving, changing*

*Gulls hymning
Across sky
Vast like
The seeking mind.
Am I what I think?
Can I become what I seek?*

*Here mind
Opens receiving
Ever changing light.
Now, time of
Allowing entrance
To the inner temple*

*Where all I love waits
Aware of living
Within the created order
With change a new beginning
Entrance beyond horizons
Into waiting peace*

Trees

Winter trees
Naked and vulnerable
Fading light
Blackbird pulsating
Stillness
Cold close and clinging
Mind calm in vastness.

Treading reverently
Sense of refuge
Still endless pulsating
Knocking at a closed door
Winter trees yearn upward
Ground draped with fallen leaves
Slowly a deepening of the coming night.

Walking

In light walking
bird song sprinkling
gentle life,
tall trees
beckoning.
One-ness here
Union with spirit
 walking slow
like in a church
vast with quietness
safe at last –
return to origin-
death
is going home
waiting
those linked by love
never passing away.
Breeze held my face
like annointing hands,
all I love
is here where mind
looses all shackles –
birds fly here, there
like searching questions
steps are made slowly here
in light walking.

Walking Quietly

Walking quietly
Aware of nature
Frail and vulnerable.
Here, there birds
Break in the fading light.
Blackbird insistently pulsating...
Mind reaches upward
As a tree yearning,
Longing and waiting
Like humanity, like me
For that point all history moves toward.

Looking up as gulls call
High in the closing light.
Here, now beyond the frailty
Away from tangled and choking
brokenness
This decimated landscape waits
Longing, yearning like a searching
question.

With Snow

With snow came a silence,
Space to look
Trees tall and still
Like ruins steeped
In their own history.
Sky grey and networked
With naked branches
The human is vulnerable,
Easily broken waiting
Like the trees...
Like all creation
For a next step
Toward history's culmination.
Birds, squirrels
All life forms seek survival
Blackbird pulsates in approaching
night,
Cold penetrates
Like a searching question.

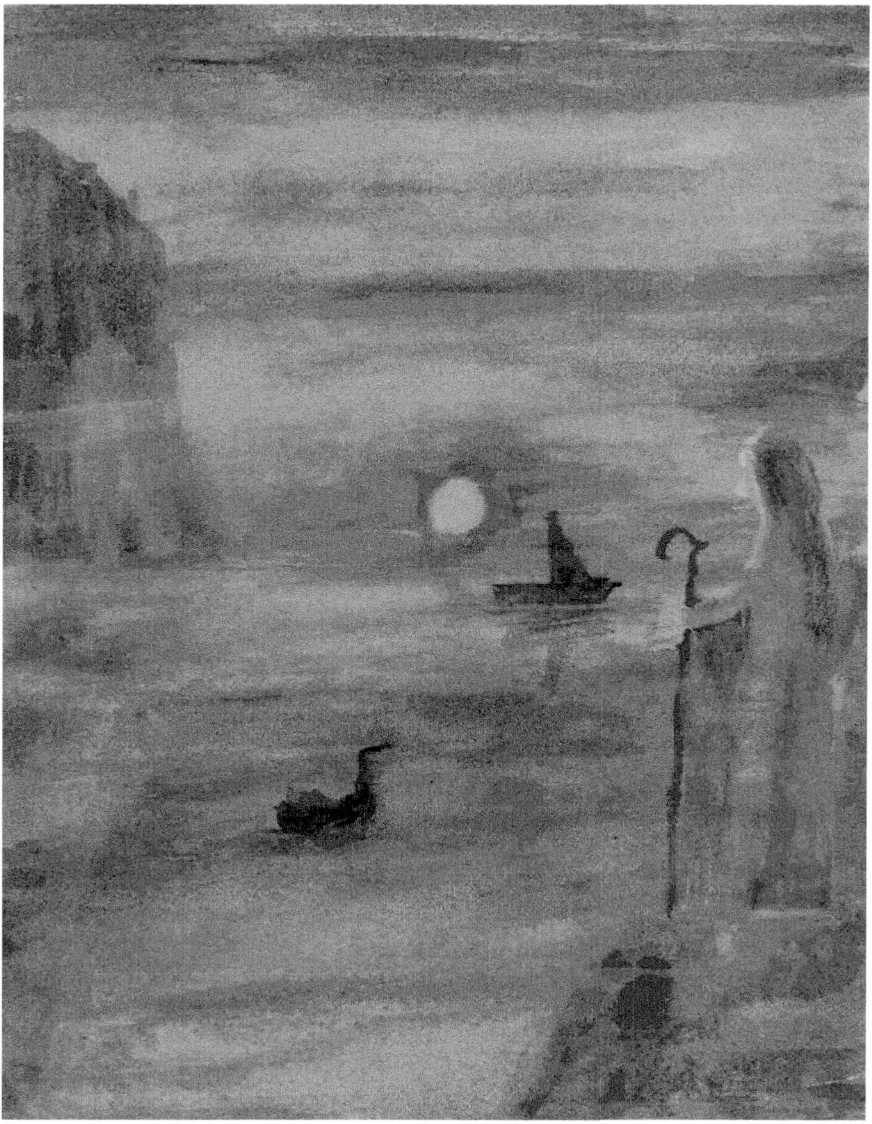

Autumn Lullaby

(For Mum)

*Sleep calm
Beloved one
This autumn
Now when
Leaves are
Falling, voices
In nature
Gently calling
Saying time
For rest
Has come
So sleep
In peace
Beloved one.
Though you
No longer
 Live this
Life you
Have gone
Into the
Blessed light
No more
Pain no
Desperate tears.
Healing, safety
Now has
Come as
You sleep
Waking in
Bliss my
Beloved one.*

For My Brother

Richard,
returned to life
closer than breathing
free at last,
end of all loneliness
end of fear
my brother near at this moment..
walls demolished...
we were not close
yet now —peace
return of years
locusts eat away

peace at last

known in local pubs,
people all around
"friendships" fragile
easily smashed
my brother cut,
wounded in his real self
looking for
what he would
never find

peace at last

now
we are brothers
in a new way
you with Mum, Dad,
all my loved ones

stay in the light
peace at last

Birds Welcome Me

(For Mum)

Birds welcome me walking
In song sprinkled light.
Cool hand of breeze
Touches my face.
Here in nature
I look for you
Free in spirit where
Shining is soft and forever.
I come to you
Down the path of tree – like
Years veined with shadows.
I look for you
Where squirrels scamper
In rain jeweled grass
Where Gulls call across
Sky vast like the mind
That finds solace in the
One life where human chains fall off
Easy and gentle as autumn leaves.

Cold Afternoon

(For Mum and Dad)

Cold afternoon,
Aware of you Mum
Closer than breathing
Here where a stone
Recalls your journey
Into the endless light.

Dad with you
Also gone into the
Clear seeing that
All life is one and
Movement toward life
Beyond reach of utterance.

COUNTRY PATH

(For Dad 15/8/05)

Country path,
Walking slowly, feet gentle
On the quiet
Road, slow, thoughtful
In holy creation
Where Mum, unseen is
Yet alive in us,
In creation as we were
Together in country peace.
Here, there break the birds,
Gentle choirs hymning
In the pure light.
So far and, we'd reach a
Bridge, look round the
Corner then calmly return.
Now, thinking of my
Dad, quietly spoken, kind,
Gentle now, gone over the bridge
Round the corner. Mum waited
In timeless higher vibration where
Now you are together, near too
In secret places of the heart
You live, holy, pure in love
In truth that shall never pass away.

HOME

(For Dad 19/8/05)

Home at last, free,
United with Mum
Where now you
Walk paths of the holy life
Together, in my heart
Where love unites us
And you both live forever
Home, where safety is
Held in universal love,
No more loneliness,
No fear, peace at
Last, I sense you
Close, aware of you
Young again, in fields
Of golden light
United in endless eternity,
Still close to me,
Still Mum and Dad, love
In truth shall never pass away.

I Come Again

(For Mum and Dad)

I come again
Here to your
Resting place.
Flowers, water,
Grass jeweled with recent
Rain. Gravestones gentle
In the autumn light.

Carnations, red, pink
White, here creation
Is holy, your gravestone
An altar. Cross near
To you speak of
Your safety resting
With Dad, peace at last.

In Spirit

In spirit,
In unending
Light, calling
I feel loved ones
In my space
Where mind opens
In quietness.

Standing again
Is in spirit
And in truth
In oneness of
Life they live
Forever

Evolve forever
In the paradise
Of wisdom
And clear seeing
Becoming jewels of
Omnipresent peace.

In secret places
Of the heart
They gather to themselves
The peace seeker
Precious one
In the eyes of God.

In Stillness

In stillness
Of the Gull hymned morning
I think of you
Mum, Dad close beside me
Now in this
Room where I rest.
Light comes
Quiet as a curious child
Whose wide eyes
Wonder at the day created
Innocent as it
Must once have been and here
Yes, here
The mind freely opens in all its
vastness,
The curtain is gently parted
And you come here
In stillness
Of the Gull hymned morning.

Now

(For Dad – 14/8/05)

Now, part of my true self
Returned to eternity,
Home, enfolded in nature
You loved – here, in still
Moments your gentle voice
Breathes, "Free at last."

Dear one, precious Dad
Back with Mum, so
Near to me – all life is
One in holy circle – gentle
Tears, yes, but light
As you both know

Joy will come – wisdom
Residing in all that is simple
Teaches again
Life is eternal
Love in truth never fades
Or passes away.

QUIET VOICE

(For Dad 27/8/05)

Now, quiet voice says, "I am free"
Gentle vibration from light beyond light
Here, as you call quietly to me.

I know the lady beside you, I see
Her looking at me with spiritual sight
Now, quiet voice says, "I am free"

No fear, end of all loneliness, tall as a tree
Reaching upward, end of all fright
Here, as you call quietly to me.

Mum, Dad forever with me
Never far, a thought away, from pure white
Now, quiet voice says, "I am free"

No more pain, no grief, eternal purity
Love never dies and knows no day or night
Here, as you call quietly to me.

Gentle man, with Mum safe in eternity
In my heart you dwell in special light
Now, quiet voice says I am free
Here as you call quietly to me.

Remembering Here

Here, by your grave
Remembering – being gathered
In love – knowing
Something of the timeless
Remembering – being your
Carer, our companionship
In suffering, offering
Service of my hands
Remembering – "special friends"
"Travelling companions"
Now, with Dad, you walk
In light living forever in
Oneness of creation
There is no ending
Just stages on a
Journey to further life
Gathered in divine abiding.

Sometimes

(For Mum)

Sometimes
I go back to
Those times
Mind journeying
Finding
You whose dear
Body
I served
With skills
Carried by my
Feeling, frail hands.
Body broken
As a stark
Winter tree
Yes,
I go back
Of course I do
To times
When special love
Made life worth living.
Now with Dad
You are both free
In spirit
Free of it all
In oneness of all life
Where true freedom is.

The Listener

Listener, there when my
First breath danced
In glory of your
Personhood.
Traveller, along my
Every road leaving
Creation signed with
Your gathering honour
From eternity your
Light walks beside me
Still, you are here.
We travelled
While arthritis, pain,
Blighted your
Dear body now, you
Are free my special
Friend is holy angel
From realms of glorious
Light, here, all sound
Speaks of love unending
Shows purity of
Light within light.

The Visit

For Eve

I find
You resting
Sunken cheeks
Tired eyes
Waiting bravely
In a quiet corner
Of the busy hospital
We talked
Your faltering voice
Spoke
As often of
Concern for others
Slowly you
Journeyed to paths
Of waiting sleep
I was able to be there.
As I left
And went out
Into the busy street
I looked up
Clouds obscured the sun.

Thinking Of Mum And Dad

(12th August 2005)

*From where I'm sitting
Here, in August,
Clear evening sky,
Garden, roof tops
Refreshed where rain
Has gently come.*

*I think of you Dad,
Now with Mum
Held in pulsating
Heart of eternity
Now, in secret shining
Lands of the heart*

*You're both together
United in love,
Living for ever
Raindrops like tears yet,
Beautified with light
Of healing, love and peace.*

White Flowers

(For Mum)

White flowers
I bring
Recalling hours
We spent together
In laughter
In tears.
White, pure
Like the gift
You gave of
Yourself, flower
Of your personhood
Unfolds now
Beautified in memory.
Seasons turn,
Warmth and calmness
Touch me here
Where you rest in
The heart of holiness
Reaching me
Quietly and in peace.

WREATH

(For Mum)

Again, with faltering hands
I place a wreath, here
Where memory glows
With your love, special friend
Gone away to the higher life.
Now, during Christmas
Our lives can blend again
Now, I know Mum, you
Dance with Dad safe, all
Tears wiped away. No more
Pain, free at last.

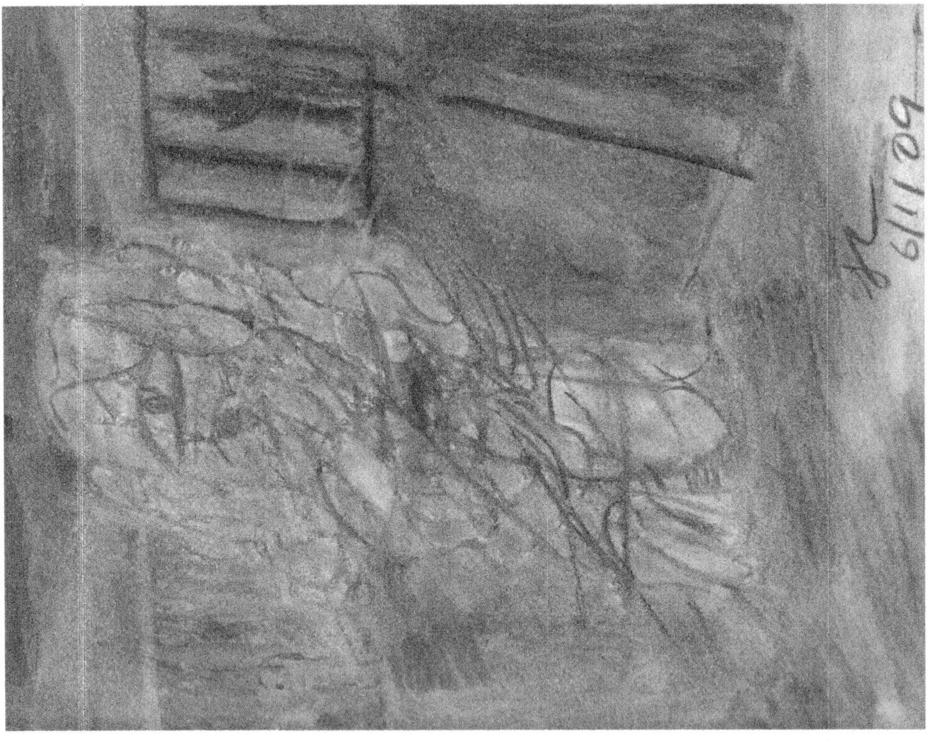

CONFLICT

Death in Autumn

(For Elkie Lee-Taylor 6/11/08)
In autumn
Frail like a fallen leaf
They took him.
Body veined with violence
Pinioned crucifixion
Like in a room
Used only for killing.
Could touches
Like a sinister hand.
Along shadowed corridors
Of time the desperate voice shrieks
"No, this is not the way!"
Silence and waiting
Then, entrance to
Death's refuge
Free at last.

Easter

Frail winter tree
Desolate branches
Oustretched
Clinging to leaf
Frail and vulnerable.
Done, at last
The finish.
Agonized falling
Broken and alone.

In my space,
My silence
He speaks in secret
Places of your
Pain and mine
"To see the light
Acknowledge darkness
Still, myself I
Pour out for you."

Freedom

Quiet,
Entry into silence
With its freedom
To share
While being alone.
Silence leads
To the horizon
Where noise
In the person ceases,
Eyes open at last
Now,
Sitting where the
Clock pulsates
Leading to contemplation,
To the way
That waits for the way things are.
This way
With eyes open
Is true and innocent reality
Where the mind
Looses all chains
Now, bird – like flying
Free, yes free at last.

Friend On Death Row

(For L.C.)

*Often, I think of you
Incarcerated
In Death Row waiting,
Always waiting
For the walk from which
None return.*

*Strapped down
Crucifixion like aware
Of the evil light
As they vein your body
With violation
Last word, final prayer*

*Will stay with some
Who weep as
You go where none
Shall harm you,
Away from this place,
Free at last.*

*I am there
Sending thought, prayer,
Feeling distance
Cannot dim the glow
Of common personhood
Filling the miles with shining.*

*Waiting, much of existence
Consists in this.
When they take you finally I
Will know and long
For peace to find you
As you walk into endless light.*

From Stillness

A clinging and cold stillness
Trees barren and broken
Contorted architecture lining
The darkening sky
Walking, aware of
People plentiful as fallen leaves
Victims of predatory forces
Gull calls across vast sky,
Heralding the path beyond
Call to see clearly
Blackbird insistent as a
Searching question...
I move on, down the years
A child runs laughing...
No fear now,
I know the child, I
Hold his hand,
From the higher life
My mother, happy as
Dancing water
Smiles as the child
Takes me into the light.

In Memoriam – Ronnie Easterbrook

*Quietly
with gathering of night
news of leaving,
Ron has gone home.
"Is it nothing to you who pass by?"
the scream evil ones wished not to hear
resonates across night unending
protest of his tortured body
flesh clinging to protuberant bone
night and death
were long time companions
during wait vulnerable
to predatory monster
watching a sick old man
rage into the fading light
"Is it nothing to you who pass by?"
Law wallows in wickedness.
abomination of desolation
where it ought not to be
ignighting flames of righteous anger
"Is it nothing to you who pass by?"
Murdering state pursued
by all unfolding truth,
evil beyond the bounds of utterance
rest in peace, soldier of humanity
gone home now far from enveloping
night
"Nothing to them that pass by"*

*here, among the cycles of nature
your memory visits –
go home quietly
return to spirit,
waiting divine abiding
Trees move in rivers*

Of wind
I whisper your honour
Now you are one
With all creation,
Death is freedom,
One with nature,
One with the vastness
Of the gull anthemed
unending sky
at peace on your journey
go home quietly Ron
Rest in Peace

Mind

Mind,
Vast, unending
A place
Of shadowed
Winter forest.
I have
Felt breaking
Fragmenting
Vicious
Hell spawned of cruelty.

Hell is
Mind made tangled.
No path
Longing for
Light yet darkness
Is sown by
Evil others.
Frail for ever...

Hell is where
Thought screams
In darkness
The truly human
Leads through hell..
Hope is the
Child lost yet

Never abandoned..
Child screaming
In agonised vibration
Of door slamming
"This is not the way,
It can never be the way"
Finding the child means looking again.

None Choose To Hear

Blackbirds herald approaching night,
I think of them captive along corridors
Of screams, none chooses to hear
Where slamming of heavy doors
Violates the frailty of those
 Pained with the weight of hours.

No, this is not the way,
Fear is not the way
Destruction of what makes me
Human can never be the way.
Through menacing solitude
The mind must be free

To weary captures with questions
As seasons turn inevitably
Watch by those far from
Any reality of a common life.
Trees yearn upward like a searching
mind
While among the imprisoned justice

Sees the lost and broken,
Sees and weeps
Feeling the vibration
Of the slammed doors
The heavy hours and calls
"Not in my name yet still none choose
to hear."

"Fitted Up"

(Remembering H.B. and all involved)

Shadows form in your face
mask behind which
true self laughs
years violated by
your betrayal
shadow of Judas
true you in
evil pretence of innocence,
constant coming to me
rendering me helpless –
institutional uniformed evil –
this is "fitting up"
this is the "field of blood"
this is shadows in your face

REFUGE

Refuge here
In my room.
Rest,
Safety watching
Light slowly
Illumine my space.
Nourished
By stillness
In the gull hymned morning
Aware again
Of the person
As vulnerable
Yet able to
Be here
Calm and alone.
Looking
At the light
Seeing, knowing
Freedom
Where the mind
Travels a
Pilgrim's path
Where shadows
Can be teachers
Of the deeper knowledge.
The true self lives
Fully here.
Outside sky is vast
Like the mind.
The waiting horizon
Is nearer each moment
As coolness anoints me
Preparing me to go on.

Shadows

Shadows
Gentle in my room
Silent
Heralds of approaching evening
Resting
Aware now of you
Dear ones
From the gathering light
Close now
Linking to me
Here in wholeness
Of the one life.
No fear
Now, end of all pain
That stalks
Predatory in tangled
Forests
Of the fragmented self.
Dear ones
Close, teaching that
With all shadows,
In time
Will come light on
The pilgrim path.

The Prisoners

Far away,
Fragile as fallen
Leaves these
The prisoners wait
Where the weight of hours
Is endless
And along deserted
Passages rages
The scream none
Want to hear.

They know too
The prison of the
Heart where
The true self
Is incarcerated.
Yet somewhere
Amid tangled branches
Struggles understanding
The voice declaring

"No! No! No!
This is not the way."
Cycles of despair and pain
Keep turning
Endlessly.
Revenge is revenge
It is not justice the
Wise one declaring
" Look with clear eyes
At the tree from whence they fell

*Let them know
Smiling in the heart,
Renewed inner life."
Results do not matter
More than truth.
Too many borders
Have been crossed too often.
Leaves of nature raped
And pillaged while
Justice the wise one cries "no.'*

The Singing

Darkness,
night without ending
vast silence
where minds
pilgrimages
looking yet
no path
is this hell?
sense of fatality

Then the singing

Waiting
where time has
passed never to return
thought is alone
in this close night
'Hypno' personifies sleep
'Thanatos' personifies death
both said in mythology
to be sons of 'Nyx'
personification of
darkness

Then the singing

Myth, a way of
saying things
uttering the unutterable
thought is alone
waiting...
a sense of singing
in darkness
gliding swan – like
to the open mind
waiting
for the other life

Then the singing

Entering
path to waiting
light
Thanatos greeted
with great joy
mind journeys
onward
seeking and finding
hell waits where it is felt
where night will end
soul opens as a flower
young in innocent shining

Then the singing...

The Victims

In light slowly fading,
Among skeletal trees
I pause, looking....
Branches frail, vulnerable
In the clinging cold
Frail fallen leaves drape
The waiting ground
Dark halls of history
Showed them
Bodies everywhere,
Bones protuberant and broken
Souls in death's other kingdom
Free at last with all the waiting eternal
Some names will always be long
shadows
Auschwitz, Treblinka, Dachau...
Yet here, in winter I honour victims
Of past and present predatory cruelty.
Darkness is drawing to itself,
The winter sun smoulders....

Those in Prison

I think of
Them
Shadowed far
From
Gentle eye
Wanting
To find true
Humanity
In the shadowed forest
Where
They wait alone.
Worse than captured
Body is
Mind held hostage
By evil in a mask deceiving
All who
Do everything but think
No, no, no,
It is not way
In the dark of
Ignorance again
Pilate washes his hands.

Time to Feel

(For R)

Unearthly silence
Skeletal trees
Frail, broken
Fallen leaves drape
The dry grass
There is a cold…

Time to feel,
In vulnerable nature
The language of pain
Bird pulsates
In coming darkness

I feel him
Helpless, strapped down
Vulnerable to
Evil terrible beyond
Faltering utterance..
Body veined

With lethal violation
Watching were eyes
Knowing fear,
The two holy ones
Truth with justice were
Strangers to judicial murder.

I recall him now,
Entering his refuge of the spirit
Cold touches me like a hand
He comes quietly here
Among the yearning trees.
Frailty and unearthly silence.

Time for Calm

Time for calm,
Noise within self
Received into this
Space created by quiet.
Clock ticks form
Gentle ripples in the
Pool of silence, stillness
Brings knowing and ripples
Move out as a seeker wanting
Light on the hard question.
In this time one can be
Still and begin to know,
To see clearly that
Light and shadow here,
In this room, make it
Part of the one life
Where illumination and darkness
Are often companions
Leading on to a greater light.

Wanting Silence

(For Reggie)

Peace,
At last glad finding
Of silence.
No harm now
There, stretched
Crucifixion like
While killers
Veined his body
Entering refuge
Where death's vast
Country is purified by tears.
Now we love more
Deeply our friend
Murdered by the state.
Love will never die
In eternity's kingdom
He stands again strong
In the unending light.

Where Does Pilate Wash His Hands?

Where does Pilate wash his hands?

Where real criminals
Hurt the hurting
Justice is prostituted to
Revenge and
Society is haunted
By screams nobody
Wants to hear.

Where police, bullying cowards
Extract confessions
Under duress, which courts, accept
Where vulnerable victims
Of corrupt system so often
Despair of living seek to snuff

Out lives frail as a candle
Flame flickering in the darkness
Of ignorance.
Pilate today is the liar, the
Betrayer deaf to all
He does not want to hear.

Where does Pilate wash his hands?

Where no sense of belonging is,
Where scapegoats of selfish class
interest
Wander lost and afraid
Where prison carried in the heart
Holds all that has died inside.
Where nobody wants clear seeing

*Eyes are not shut
No fingers in ears
Yet, nobody wants to
Hear or see.
No community only
Long shadows
That don't belong.*

*Where does Pilate wash his hands?
Where they become dirty again and again*

SAFE

1

Sleep – at last
Safety – at last
Peace – at the last

going to interface
between
sleeping and waking
life and
the further life

time
yields an appointed time
my
passing will be
a quest

into
other reality
good
I can sleep
in safety
window open

skin
soft breeze
anointing
my
waiting body
then waking

each
gull anthemed
morning

*seeing time
coming
when angel loved ones*

*ferry
my soul,
my true self
beyond
the horizon
ever closer*

*than breathing
Mum, Dad
Granny, Granddad
Richard
my
brother*

*all loved
ones live
differently
no
real
separation*

*My death
is the journey out
I long for
sleep finding
deeper awakening
in the one life*

2

*The appointed
time waits as a wise
one,
companion in
the valley of
shadow*

*here
where the pilgrim
soul
journeys sharing
treasures
from its*

*path
where, on the
cross roads
showing
the paths from
endless shadow
A child
innocent, lost
runs screaming, cast out
by
evil in many forms*

3

life
whole life
entry into
one life
of the created
order

needs
innocence, needs
the wise one
holding
the cord of love
linking

to beyond
the horizon
where
like a waiting
treasure is
the divine abiding

4

*my lady
of silence be
the source
of all we share
one creation
reaches out*

*like a
yearning
tree
for no sound
only
that beyond
human hearing*

*my lady
of silence loose
all shackles
of ignorance,
of fear
restore*

*Humanity
broken like glass
yet in
each piece
wantonly discarded
find again the true light*

*take us
to freedom
loosed from the
great evil
the predatory
silence of friends*

Printed in Great Britain
by Amazon